CINCINNATI

By
Jim Borgman

*MERRY CHRISTMAS,
JOE!*

JIMBORGMAN
1992

With an introduction by
Edie Magnus

Production by
Lynn Goodwin Borgman

Design by
Rob Schuster

CREDITS
Kathy Doane: Copy editing
Robert A. Flischel: Portrait photograph on back cover
Michael E. Keating: Cover photography
Carol Schuster and Ron Cosby: Production

SPECIAL THANKS TO
Photography Department of the
The Cincinnati Enquirer
George Blake
Harry Whipple
Skip Merten

PUBLISHED BY
Colloquial Books
P.O. Box 20045
Cincinnati, Ohio 45220

ISBN 0-9609632-4-3

Library of Congress Catalog Card Number: 92-074301

CONTENTS

INTRODUCTION

I have finally figured out why I have never been the subject of a Jim Borgman cartoon.

Because his drawings are done in black and white. And he would definitely have to color me green.

Yes, that's green with envy. I mean, really. Just look at what Jim can do with a few zoop-de-zoops of the hand. (Since I'm in television, and we constantly erode the English language anyway, I figure you'll know what zoop-de-zoop means!)

Writing news stories is such an excruciating process. We sit, stare, sweat or swear at the keyboard. Searching for the right words, the right feeling, the right balance, the right perspective. Whether it's to make a dull story interesting, or a complicated one simple and concise, it is ultimately exasperating and often leaves you ready to tear your hair out.

Enter Jim Borgman who can tell that same story in a way that takes your breath away. Like Pete. And the 911 operator. And Robert Mapplethorpe. And judging from his photograph, Jim's not tearing his hair out, either!

If it is true that a picture is worth a thousand words, I'd like to suggest a corollary: One cartoon is worth a thousand moving pictures. So many images cross our consciousness each day: Angry consumers, grieving families, not-so-politic politicians, the children who are starving faraway and here at home. I wonder if the "electronic village" actually threatens to dull our senses with visual overload.

But just at that moment when we're tempted to turn it all away, comes a drawing that can capture the essence of a thing, that can force us to re-engage. Jim Borgman is awfully good at that. His vision of the events in our world shines through like a light.

And if the drawings themselves aren't enough to admire, consider the man. Jim's always been unflinching in taking a hard look at the problems facing Cincinnati. But he's also been unfailing in his love and support for the city. That's a rare combination. A gift which he gives back every day. A gift which everyone who sees *Jim Borgman's Cincinnati* will appreciate.

I'm glad this book is coming out because I don't get to see Borgman cartoons as regularly as I did when I lived in Cincinnati. Still, Mom and Dad send them to me often. And when they arrive, I briefly convulse with feelings of wonder, amusement and (this is the last time I will admit this) envy.

It's a good thing those TV cameras can make color corrections when you look a little green.

Edie Magnus

Edie Magnus, former Channel 12 news anchor, is now Health and Medical correspondent for CBS News.

RAISING LAZARUS FROM THE DEAD

THIRTY SECON

CINCINNATI

OVER THE RHINE...

OAKLEY FOREST PARK
MADEIRA DELHI
HYDE PARK
PRICE HILL
TERRACE PARK
WINTON WOODS
FINNEYTOWN
SEDAMSVILLE
MT. ADAMS
MT. AUBURN
KENNEDY HTS.
MT. AIRY

FRANK... CALL WHEN YOU
...A CALL
...ANCE A 21...YOU
...FRANK CALLING...

ENQUIRER

Ich Bin Ein Cincinnatian

When I was a Price Hill 7 year-old, the Berlin Wall went up in Germany as the Iron Curtain rose all across Eastern Europe. My dad, trying to explain what was happening in a way that I could grasp, said it would be as if a great wall ran the length of Vine Street, dividing east from west Cincinnati. Uncrossable. Guards ready to shoot anyone who tried.

I missed the metaphor. It would be years before I realized there wasn't a wall down the middle of Vine Street. Then more years before I realized I had it right the first time. I didn't lay eyes on Hyde Park Square until I was 22.

When the Berlin Wall came back down, my childhood image was perfect for this series of cartoons.

"To be continued...?" We were off on a weeklong adventure.

THE WALL.

20 MILES LONG, 20 FEET HIGH,
200 YEARS THICK.

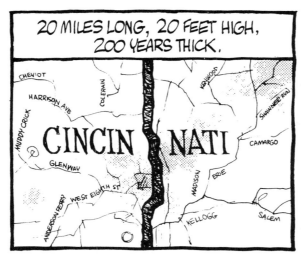

RUNNING ALONG THE MIDDLE OF VINE STREET
FROM THE BELTWAY TO THE RIVER, THE
WALL HAD DIVIDED THE WEST SIDE OF CINCINNATI
FROM THE EAST SIDE FOR AS LONG AS ANYONE
COULD REMEMBER.

LEGEND HELD THAT IT HAD GONE UP OVERNIGHT
WHEN YOUNG GRANDIN KILGOUR ABANDONED HIS
POST AT THE UBER·DER·VIADUCT BREWERY TO GO
BARHOPPING IN MT. ADAMS.

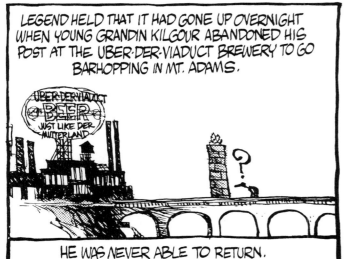

HE WAS NEVER ABLE TO RETURN.

THAT WAS A LONG TIME AGO.
AND SINCE THAT DAY, CINCINNATI FAMILIES HAVE BEEN DIVIDED —
BROTHER FROM BROTHER, FATHER FROM DAUGHTER, MATRON FROM MAID.

... AS FOR YOUNG KILGOUR,
HE OPENED A COFFEE
EMPORIUM AND BECAME
FAMOUS ACROSS HYDE PARK
FOR HIS CAPPUCCINO AU LAIT.

TO BE CONTINUED.

Having lived about an equal number of years on each side of our wall, I felt qualified to go after our cultural differences.

OH, THERE WERE DEFECTIONS FROM TIME TO TIME....

...SOME EVEN SURVIVED.

THERE WERE RUMORS OF A SETON GRAD WORKING THE WEEKEND SHIFT AT TALBOTS.

A FORMER WAITRESS AT MAURY'S TINY COVE WAS SAID TO HAVE A SMALL CATERING BUSINESS IN KENWOOD.

CROISSANTS 'Я' US

GOETTA
SCHNITZEL
CHILI – W/CHEESE

SUNSET AVE.

A PROMINENT CONCEPTUAL ARTIST FLED MT. ADAMS FOR THE BOHEMIAN SIDE STREETS OF PRICE HILL.

JIM BORGMAN
CINCINNATI
ENQUIRER 1990

AND THE OLDTIMERS WHO GATHERED AT THE GLENWAY HARDEE'S FOR BREAKFAST LIKED TO TELL THE TALE OF THE KID WHO'D WORN A RALPH LAUREN POLO SHIRT TO A TAILGATE PARTY BEFORE THE ELDER-WEST HI GAME IN '82.

HE WAS SHOT ON THE SPOT.

MUSTANGS

...AND HIS BODY WAS NEVER FOUND!

TO BE CONTINUED.

THE ONLY POINT OF LEGAL PASSAGE THROUGH THE WALL WAS KNOWN AS 'CHECKPOINT CHARLIELUKEN.'

WESTWOOD | E. WALNUT HILLS

IT WAS NAMED AFTER THE SON OF THE ONLY MAN EVER TO SURFACE PUBLICLY IN BOTH HALVES OF THE DIVIDED CITY.

A VISA WAS REQUIRED WHEN TRAVELING FROM EAST TO WEST....

.... AN AMERICAN EXPRESS GOLD CARD WHEN TRAVELING WEST TO EAST.

THE WESTERN SIDE OF THE WALL WAS FESTOONED WITH SPORTS SLOGANS AND HIGH SCHOOL EPITHETS....

JIM BORGMAN
CINCINNATI ENQUIRER 1990

....EASTSIDERS PREFERRED ROOKWOOD TILES AND THE CUTEST LITTLE INLAID BRIC·A·BRAC.

BUT HISTORY WAS CONSPIRING AGAINST THE WALL.

VINE ST.

TO BE CONTINUED.

By about this time, I was receiving phone calls from Delhi to Madeira with the same complaint: "You're being unfair to our side!"

11

When all is said and done, Gorbachev would have less of an identity crisis settling in California than most of us would have moving across town.

" IT WAS ANNOUNCED TODAY IN STOCKHOLM THAT WALTER PFLEGELMAN OF PRICE HILL HAS BEEN AWARDED THE 1989 NOBEL PRIZE IN BOWLING...."

I enjoy caricaturing Cincinnati archetypes. These folks are straight out of my childhood. I still can hear Jack Moran's whispering commentary on the "Hoinke Classic."

13

"SINCE WHEN DO THEY PUT BAMBOO SHOOTS AND ALFALFA SPROUTS ON A 4-WAY?!"

Heart Healthy Chili? This news item was merely an excuse to draw a unique Cincinnati scene.

HARRY SNODGRASS, LATE-BLOOMING POLITICAL ACTIVIST

FEDERAL LEGISLATION LIMITING THE LENGTH OF VISITS FROM OUT-OF-TOWN RELATIVES

PLEASE SIGN

" IT'S CALLED THE PORKOPOLIS DIET ... I AVOID OKTOBERFEST, SUMMERFAIR AND 'A TASTE OF CINCINNATI' AND LOSE TWENTY POUNDS A YEAR."

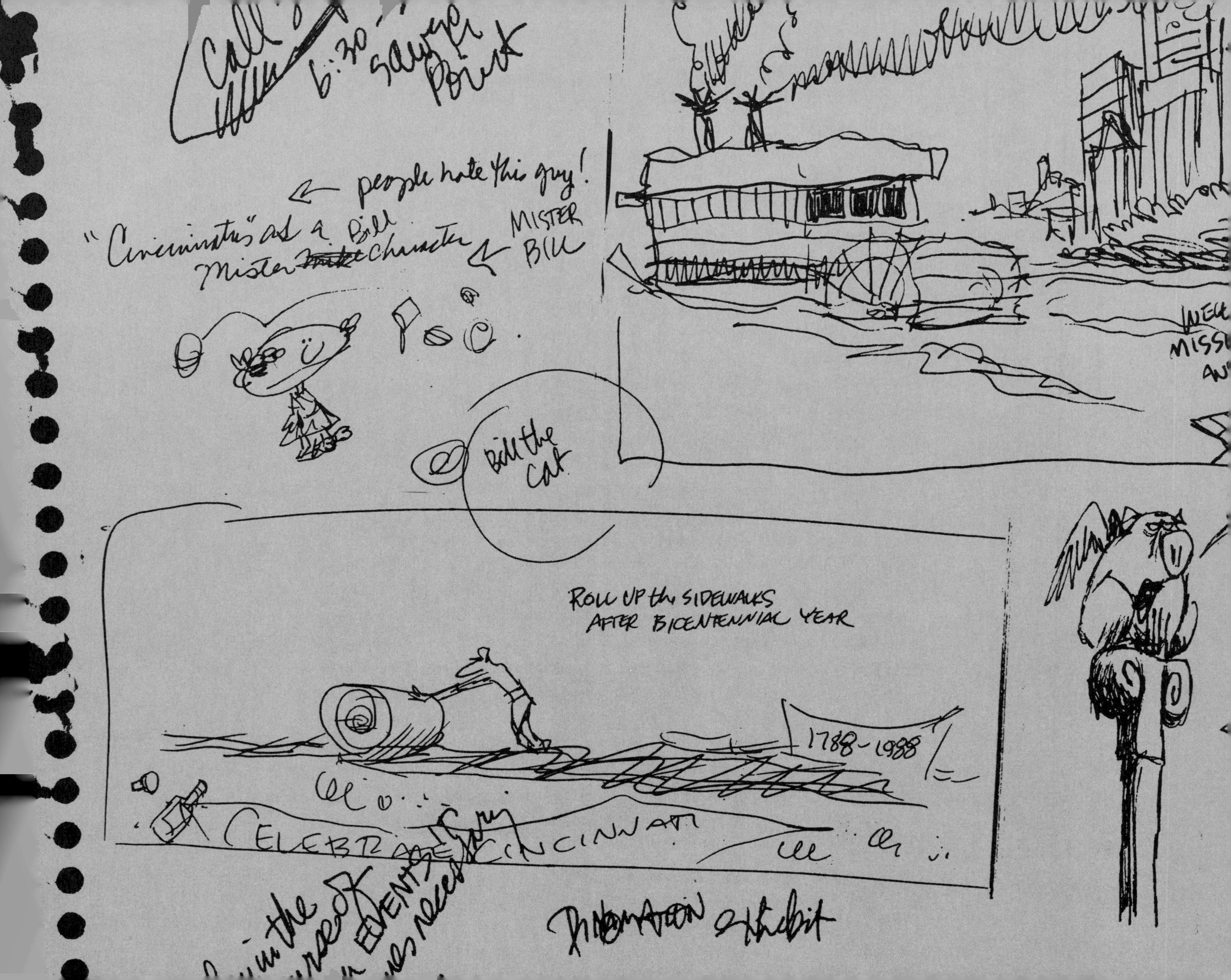

Call
6:30 Sawyer Point
people hate this guy!
"Cincinnatus" as a Bill Mister character
MISTER BILL
Bill the Cat
ROLL UP the SIDEWALKS AFTER BICENTENNIAL YEAR
1788–1988
CELEBRATE CINCINNATI

Cincinnati Turns 200

When my office at *The Enquirer* used to look out on Vine Street, I could sometimes squinch my eyes and almost see the street as it appeared a century ago... pigs running wild on their way to the slaughterhouses.

What a time to be a cartoonist in Cincinnati! Imagine the corpulent William Howard Taft actually climbing the hill of the street that now bears his name. Or our ancestors wading across the Ohio River in the dead of the night, watching for lantern codes from the north bank, signaling freedom.

Why did Adams get to be a Mount but Price only a Hill? And don't you wonder whatever happened to the elms, sycamores, walnuts and vines that gave identities to downtown's streets? If there were ever plums on Plum Street, they have long since turned to prunes and ensconced themselves in the bowels of City Hall as our public servants.

It's a rich history, and we celebrated it big time during our Bicentennial year. Pigs even sprouted wings for the occasion.

"MAYBE I'M GETTIN' OLD....BUT BACK IN MY NEW YORK DAYS THEY SENT FIGHTER PLANES AFTER ME..."

You could tell it would be an unusual year. One day we woke up to find a giant inflatable King Kong perched on the side of the Carew Tower.

One of the city's more important debates involved the placement of tiny winged pigs atop a proposed bicentennial sculpture, a lighthearted reference to our porkopolis days.

"PEOPLE NEVER HAVE WARMED UP TO THAT BICENTENNIAL MASCOT, HAVE THEY...?"

"Cincinnatus," a doughy, Ziggyish character,
was christened the official host of the celebration.
He became the mascot people loved to hate.

CINCINNATI at 100

CINCINNATI at 200

A curious message-board robot settled itself outside the
Contemporary Arts Center, filling a place in our hearts previously
held by that grooved, granite paperweight, "Law and Society".

1988 ALL-STARS

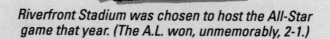

Riverfront Stadium was chosen to host the All-Star game that year. (The A.L. won, unmemorably, 2-1.)

"RUMORS OF OUR DEATHS HAVE BEEN GREATLY EXAGGERATED...."

The most impressive event of the year celebrated our riverboat heritage — a gathering of tall stacks right out of Huckleberry Finn...

POST-TRAUMATIC BIRTHDAY SYNDROME

A Day in the Life

I read the news today, oh boy. 4,000 holes in Interstate-75.

All cities have the same gamut of issues and problems as Cincinnati, I suppose. But ours seem so quirky. We imploded a college dorm? A cop was caught mooning from his cruiser? We get rid of our pigeons by breeding falcons on downtown rooftops...to prey on them? We explode our bridges?

It's e-e-e-e-e-eleven o'clock and time to find out what's been happening in your wacky town.

Here's a traffic watch update: AAAAUGGGH!

On the editorial page, we typically debate arms control and the national debt. But sometimes we have to leave our ivory tower and talk about what's really on everybody's mind...

"IS IT ME, OR DO THE POTHOLES SEEM WORSE THIS YEAR?"

"IT'S OK, DEAR.... HIS PAPERS SEEM TO BE IN ORDER."

...like surviving a harrowing commute...

"WAKE UP, DEAR.... I THINK I HEAR THE TRAFFIC STARTING TO MOVE AGAIN."

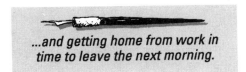

...and getting home from work in time to leave the next morning.

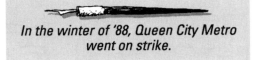

In the winter of '88, Queen City Metro went on strike.

"YOU KNOW, ALMA, THIS BUS STRIKE IS REALLY BEGINNING TO FROST MY SHORTS..."

"I WAS JUST ABOUT TO SAY, 'WHAT NEXT?!'"

HIGH HOOPS

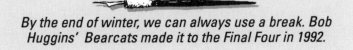

By the end of winter, we can always use a break. Bob Huggins' Bearcats made it to the Final Four in 1992.

"THINGS SURE HAVE CHANGED AROUND HERE SINCE THE MOVIES CAME TO TOWN..."

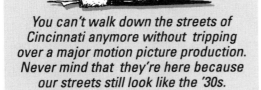

You can't walk down the streets of Cincinnati anymore without tripping over a major motion picture production. Never mind that they're here because our streets still look like the '30s.

"FRIGLEY'S BEEN IMPOSSIBLE TO LIVE WITH SINCE HE PLAYED A DOORMAN IN THE JOHN SAYLES MOVIE."

New *Cincinnati* TOURIST ATTRACTION

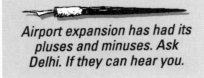

Airport expansion has had its pluses and minuses. Ask Delhi. If they can hear you.

" AH, THINK OF IT ..... CINCINNATI IN THE SPRINGTIME! "

THIS WEEK'S HIGHLIGHT:
STANDING ROOM ONLY AT DELHI COLISEUM

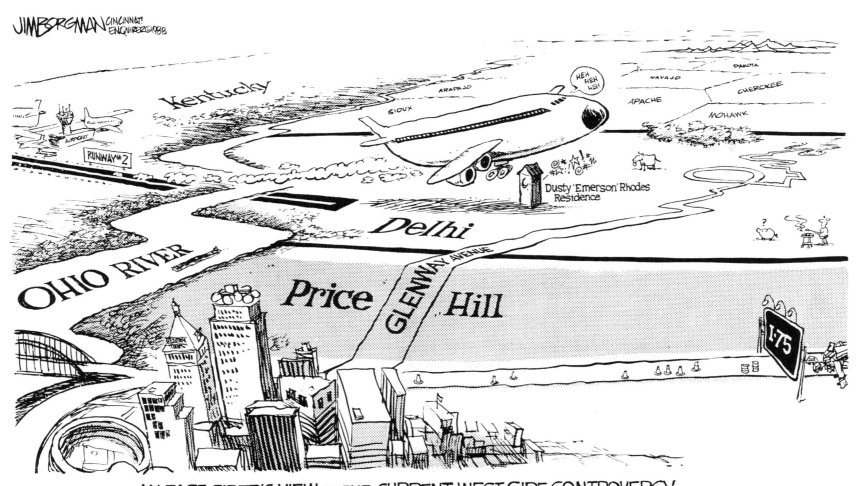

AN EAST-SIDER'S VIEW OF THE CURRENT WEST-SIDE CONTROVERSY

The dramatic implosion of the universally maligned
Sander Hall provided a cathartic moment for UC grads...

Collapsing CINCINNATI

SANDER HALL

SEWER SYSTEM

CENTRAL BRIDGE

SOCIAL NET

JIM BORGMAN
CINCINNATI
ENQUIRER©1992

...but, with budget shortfalls, it sometimes seemed as if everything was falling down around our ears.

One of the great rescue efforts in our city's lifetime
was the saving of Union Terminal from extinction...

...and inaugurating it as a new museum complex
with a spectacular Dinomation exhibit.

Other cultural institutions struggled to survive...

"SO LET'S GET ON WITH IT, HAMLET!"

...sometimes with Shakespearean flair: Out, out
damn Walnut Street Garage!

"TAKE CARE OF YOURSELVES... AND EACH OTHER."

A day in the life of Cincinnati can bring ugliness and heartache, too. Gang violence has become a reality here.

FIREWORKS

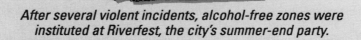

After several violent incidents, alcohol-free zones were instituted at Riverfest, the city's summer-end party.

An extra hug for Jenny

"VICE SQUAD!......OH, HI FELLAS....."

Did we get that right? A cop was caught mooning folks from his cruiser? About the same time, on-duty officers were discovered partying which put Chief Larry Whalen in the hot seat.

....CHIEF WHALEN DECLINED TO COMMENT.

Channel 9's I-Team seemed to catch all sorts of public employees sleeping on the job. This was especially inconvenient for CG&E, which was asking for a rate hike at the time.

Several serious delays and bungles caused controversy over the operation of 911 in Cincinnati. The real emergency turned out to be a lack of operator training.

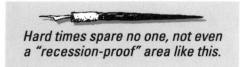

Hard times spare no one, not even a "recession-proof" area like this.

LAZARUS RAISING FEDERATED FROM THE DEAD

"MAGIC DUST?... YOU WOULDN'T PUT ME ON, NOW...?"

"I HOPE WE DIDN'T SEND ALL THE PEANUT BUTTER AND JELLY TO UKRAINE......."

Despite the recession, we sent vast shipments of peanut butter, jelly
and bread (and assembly instructions) to our Soviet sister city, Kharkiv.
But secretly, we wondered if we might soon be eating borscht.

NO ROOM AT THE INN

The legality of Christmas displays in public places was questioned. Somehow Krohn seemed empty without sheep.

"I HATE TO BREAK IT TO YOU, HARRY, BUT THERE IS NO LIST OF OFFICE CLOSINGS...."

Is Anyone in Charge Here?

"Two THUMBS UP for 'The Movies'!!"
—City of Cincinnati

Cincinnati is run by what is called the "Weak Mayor" form of government, (a title remarkable for its candor, don't you think?) The mayor is so weak, in fact, that average citizens are invited to give him a good shove when they pass him on the street. This was particularly fun in the case of Dave Mann.

No, really, the concept goes like this: a weak mayor cannot create the patronage network which so utterly corrupts other forms of government (i.e., county politics), thereby keeping the city as pure as the driven snow under the watch of the city manager. And leaving city council free to pursue re-election year-round.

The city manager then has a chance to exhibit real leadership, except that at the first sign of doing so, city council gets rid of him faster than bumper stickers at a parish festival.

City government continues to be the source of our area's richest characters. Now that there are term limits, we can expect a fresh new crop every couple years.

For years, Cincinnati ignored the obvious way of electing mayors
and let city council coalitions do the choosing. With several parties
to satisfy, the mayoralty changed hands every 25 minutes or so.

RADICAL NEW CONCEPT SHAKES CITY

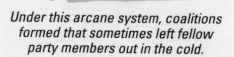

Under this arcane system, coalitions formed that sometimes left fellow party members out in the cold.

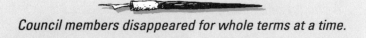

Council members disappeared for whole terms at a time.

"UM... EXCUSE US WHILE WE GO POWDER OUR NOSES."

A change of one seat could destroy a ruling coalition faster than an Israeli election. I loved drawing Bobbie Stern when she disrupted the all-male council in 1987.

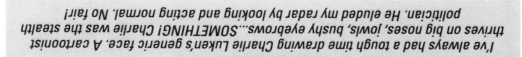

I've always had a tough time drawing Charlie Luken's generic face. A cartoonist thrives on big noses, jowls, bushy eyebrows...SOMETHING! Charlie was the stealth politician. He eluded my radar by looking and acting normal. No fair!

TOP
There were some politicians, however, who compensated with hairbrained proposals...

BOTTOM
...others who just showed up so often they became like furniture.

"... AND WHEN YOU'RE FINISHED WITH THAT, MR. MIRLISENA, THE DOG COULD USE A GOOD BATH."

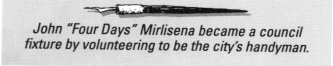

John "Four Days" Mirlisena became a council fixture by volunteering to be the city's handyman.

"IN THE FUTURE, MR. WILLIAMS, I'D SUGGEST YOU REMOVE YOUR CLEATS BEFORE YOU TALK AT COUNCIL MEETINGS..."

When Arn Bortz left council, Bengal linebacker Reggie Williams was appointed to fill his seat, which he did with all the grace of a blind-side tackle.

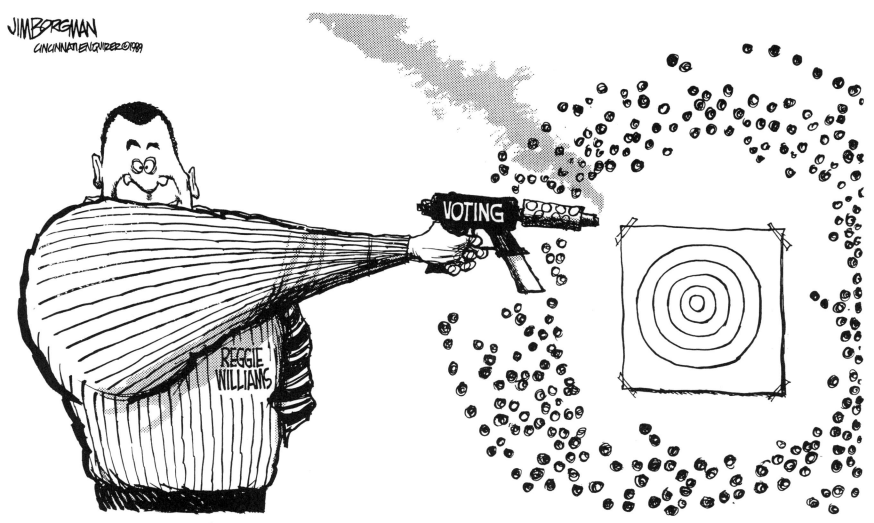

"OK, OK.... I'M STARTING TO GET THE HANG OF IT...."

Williams blew an important council vote on automatic
weapons. Perhaps he lacked practice. Councilman Williams,
it turned out, had never registered to vote in his life.

ELEPHANT GRAVEYARD

For crossing Republican Ralph Kohnen on a development vote, council's elder statesman, Guy Guckenberger, was banished from the party...

...and finished higher than ever in the subsequent election. Kohnen the Barbarian was out before long.

"I'M GOING TO GO VOTE FOR GUY GUCKENBERGER BEFORE THEY OUTLAW IT....."

Voters focused their frustration in the form of a term-limits proposal which passed, sending some familiar faces in search of a new home.

"BECAUSE YOU KEEP ELECTING THE WRONG PEOPLE, FOOL!"

Nick Vehr, who sponsored the term-limit proposal, lost the
battle for election to council but won the war by assuring
plenty of open seats in the years ahead.

When the dust settled, Dwight Tillery was the astonished new mayor. He was so new on city council that I had never drawn him before. I spent the day searching for photos to draw from.

With son, Charlie, in Washington to carry the family mantle, party chairman Tom Luken labored to revive the local Democrats.

From the day he is hired, he knows he'll be fired. With nine contrary bosses, the city manager's lot is a nasty one.

Stoic Scott Johnson's undoing was news footage of napping pothole repair crews. A number of city projects seemed to be in the doldrums.

There's always some crazy development plan on
the city's drawing board. Remember this one?

Meanwhile, the real drudge work went undone.

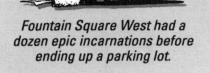

Fountain Square West had a dozen epic incarnations before ending up a parking lot.

"I GOT THE IDEA BY COMBINING ALL THE *PREVIOUS* PLANS FOR FOUNTAIN SQUARE WEST."

"OH, SURE, WE'VE HAD OUR MOMENTS OF FRUSTRATION...."

CINCINNATI ESTABLISHES A DOWNTOWN 'ENTERTAINMENT DISTRICT'

Are we having fun yet?

81

CHOOSE the REAL SEAT OF POWER in AMERICA

Congressman Charlie Luken abruptly announced that he missed his family and wouldn't run for re-election.

"WHY DO THEY HAVE TO WANT NOT TO RUN BEFORE I WANT TO VOTE FOR THEM?"

"HONEY, I BLEW UP THE DEMOCRATS!"

In the ensuing melee, David Mann emerged as the Democratic nominee to run against...uh...nobody. The Republicans fumbled their candidate in the political opportunity of a generation.

The Weather and Other Unnatural Acts

For those new to this area, we'd better warn you that Cincinnati is regularly invaded. It happens every 17 years. Swarms and swarms of little ugly, red-eyed, clicking, whirling, whizzing creatures with nothing on their nasty little minds but a wild fling before they die.

I am referring, of course, to the National Square Dancers Convention.

No, I'm not. I am referring to the cicadas, our wierd mutant visitors whose hormones so dominate their brief daylight existence that God didn't even bother to give them mouths. But for that, they behave remarkably like teen-agers at Kings Island on a hot summer night.

Between cicada invasions, we live in mortal fear of snow, pausing from this obsession only long enough to reminisce fondly about the "much deeper" drifts of our youth.

Oh, yeah, and there is this persistent rumor of humidity.

These days it snows more often on Opening
Day than on Christmas. Must be that volcano.

"OH, DON'T BE DRAMATIC, MERLE ..... EVERYBODY'S HOT."

On these 3H days (hazy, hot and humid), forget
cartooning about the federal deficit. We become
a city full of one-track minds.

Tips for SURVIVING an EARTHQUAKE

① ANIMALS HAVE HIGHLY-EVOLVED SENSES which MAY PROVIDE WARNING SIGNALS in the event of an EMERGENCY!

The OHIO EARTHQUAKE COUNCIL SUGGESTS YOU WATCH your CAT for PECULIAR BEHAVIOR ....

② ...IF IT DROPS into a WIDENING HORIZONTAL CHASM, YOU MAY BE EXPERIENCING an EARTHQUAKE.

TOP
A few years ago, a noted seismologist and insurance tycoon, Iben "the terrible" Browning, gave us time, date and location of a massive tremor that had our number on it.

BOTTOM
Nothing, uh, happened...but there were numerous reports of wild insurance agents who howled all night.

" IRVING IS SO JITTERY ABOUT THE QUAKE, I'M AFRAID I'LL HAVE TO INFORM HIM IF WE HAVE ONE..."

When the cicadas hit town, it's an event of biblical
proportions. We're talking Old Testament here.
Plagues and infestations. Oliver Stone material.

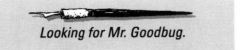

Looking for Mr. Goodbug.

"WHERE ARE ALL THE GOOD CICADAS, CAROLYN?..... EVERY DATE I GET, IT'S JUST SEX, SEX, SEX AND THEN THEY DROP DEAD."

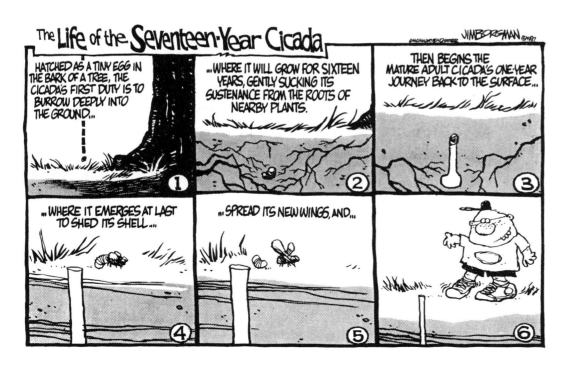

"I THINK I LIKED THE PIGEONS BETTER!"

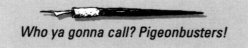

Who ya gonna call? Pigeonbusters!

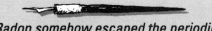

Radon somehow escaped the periodic table and got into our basements when we weren't looking. I can't find my flashlight but my fuse box glows in the dark.

"MAYBE WE SHOULD GET THE BASEMENT CHECKED FOR RADON GAS...... I JUST GOT A CHEST X-RAY FROM CHANGING THE FURNACE FILTER."

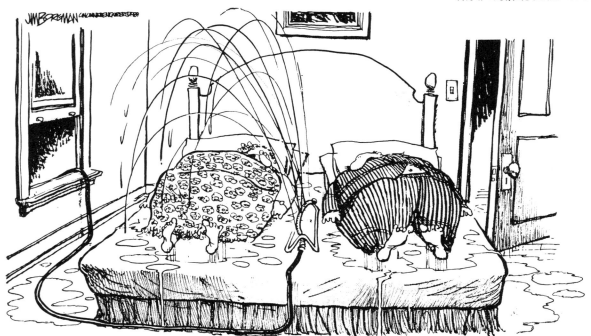

"OH FOR GOSHSAKES, IRVIN, LET'S JUST SPRING FOR A LOUSY AIR CONDITIONER!"

"OH, KNOCK IT OFF, IRVIN ...... EVERYBODY'S HOT..."

OK, so it's not too profound. But, dang, it's hot!

The Hunt for Reds October

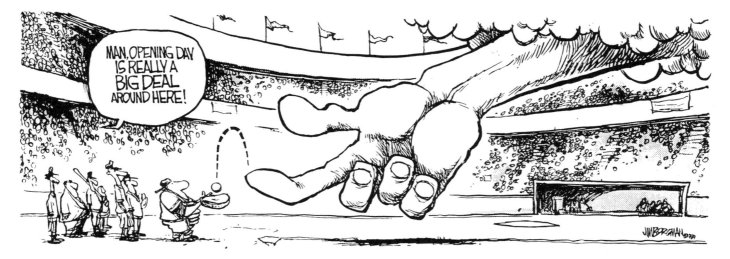

When you grow up in Cincinnati, baseball is a metaphor for life. I grew up in Price Hill throwing a rubber ball against a stone wall on our street, a number 46 (Jim Maloney) slowly unraveling from the place on my T-shirt where my mom had lovingly stitched it. I still compare my cartoons to fastballs, knucklers and, alas, slow hanging curves.

For many of us, the flavor of any particular year in our memory is colored by how the Reds played. The mid-'80's of my own life have the feeling of a Paul Householder at-bat. And even today when I come across one of my old cartoons, I can often hear Marty's voice calling the game I was listening to when I drew it.

As an editorial cartoonist, the Pete Rose gambling story should have been red meat for me. But it wasn't. Behind every line I drew chronicling his downfall was the breaking heart of the West-Side kid throwing the rubber ball.

Maybe we all assign our hearts to some team to carry our hopes and dreams along. Well, this one belongs to the Reds.

As a Cincinnatian, I'll draw almost anything to amuse myself through the toughest month of the year. I climb the walls until the pitchers and catchers report to Florida.

February in Cincinnati is what separates the men from the boys. The men turn into couch potatoes, but the boys and girls oil up their baseball gloves.

"SORRY, SCHOTTZIE, BUT RULES ARE RULES."

Love them or hate them, Marge and Schottzie are authentic Cincinnati characters. I've watched Marge sign her paw-print autograph for dozens of kids from her seat by the dugout.

"WELL, ONE GOOD THING ABOUT KEEPING THE OLD SCOREBOARD — AT LEAST WE CAN STILL HAVE SCHOTTZIE OPERATE IT.."

At a little exhibit of my cartoons once, Marge commented to one woman, "I just met him, and he isn't nearly as bad a guy as you'd think." That woman was my wife, Lynn.

There's a parking space reserved for the Big Red Machine at Cooperstown. Bench and Morgan were shoo-ins, and Tony Perez is on the threshhold.

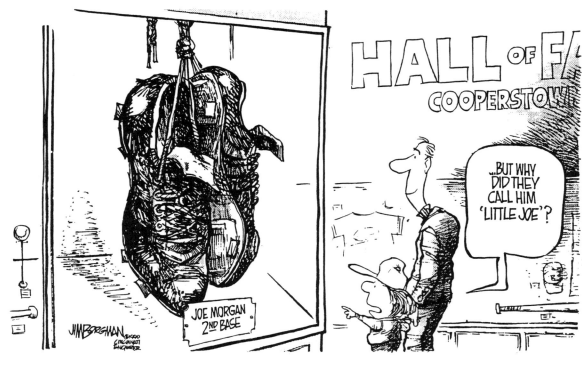

"HEY! HOW ABOUT AN AUTOGRAPH?!"

The foreshadowing of Rose's downfall came when the player-manager got into a shoving match with umpire Dave Pallone. New commissioner A. Bartlett Giamatti suspended Rose for a shocking 30 days.

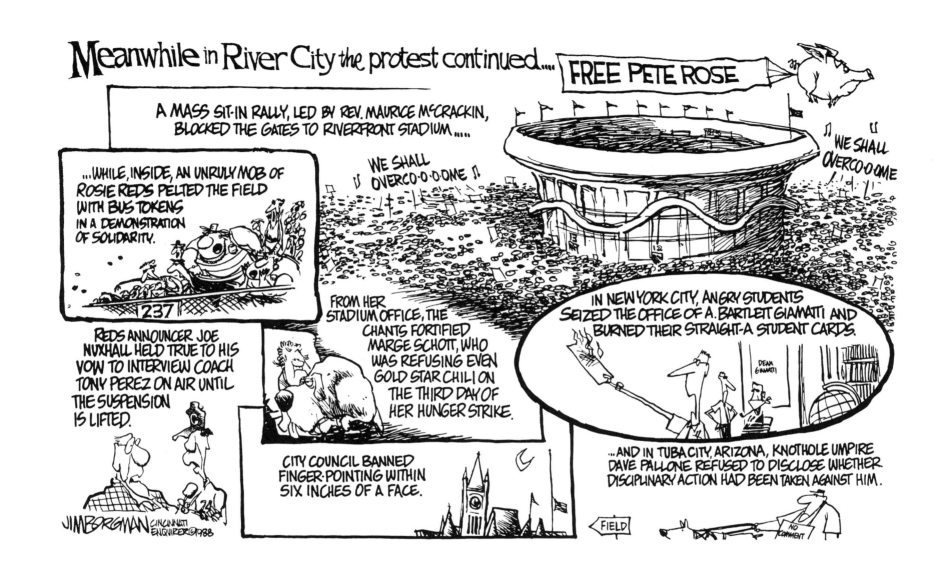

The severity of the suspension outraged the whole town. It would not be the last time the airwaves would buzz with passion over Pete.

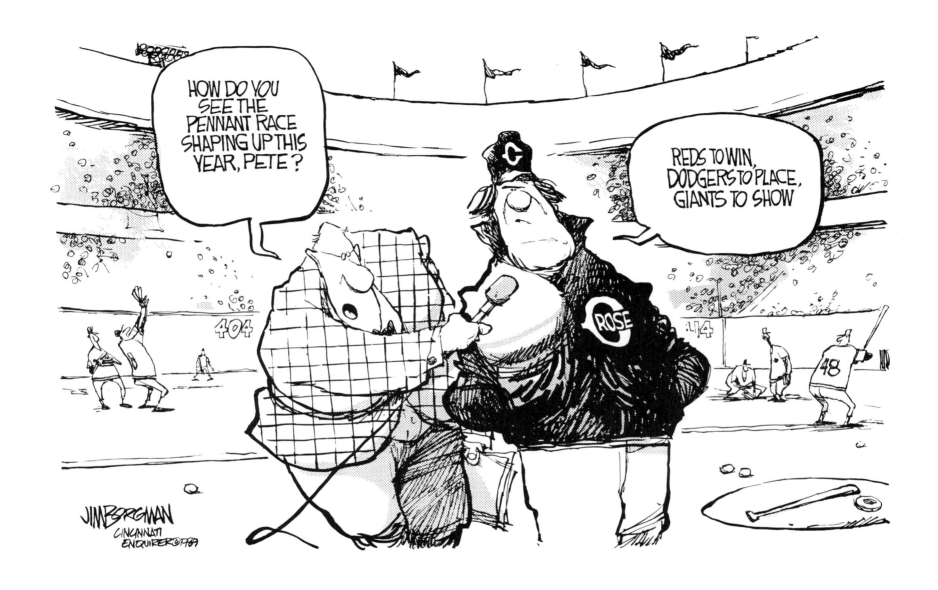

Sports Illustrated *broke the story that the office of the baseball commissioner was investigating Rose for allegedly betting on baseball.*

We sometimes forget that when the dust settled, it was tax evasion, not gambling, that landed Rose behind bars.

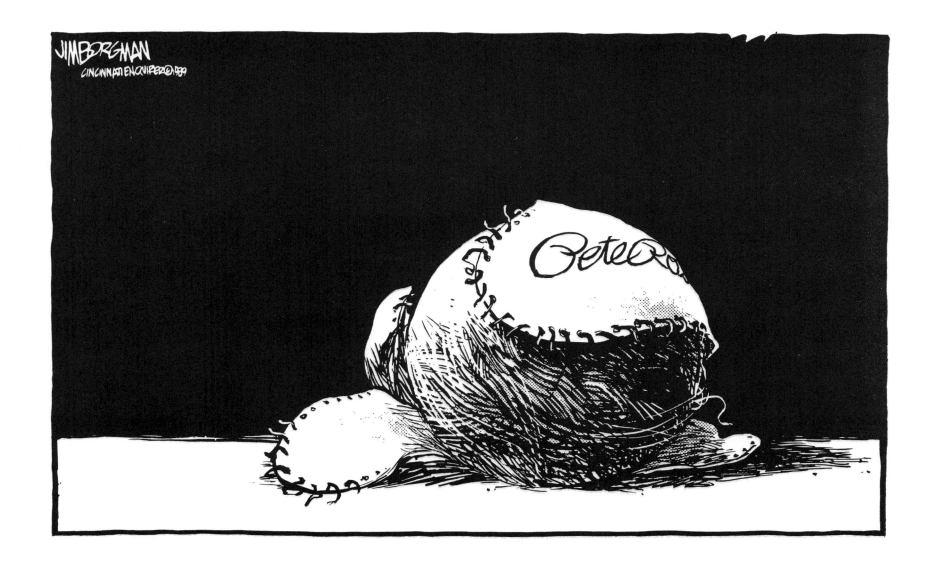

"FIRST OF ALL, SORRY ABOUT YOUR RED CARPET...."

ALL-STAR GAME
BALL
1970

WORLD SERIES MVP
BALL
1975

HIT #4192
BALL
1985

HALL OF FAME
BLACKBALL
1991

*Ultimately, the commissioner was able to take the
vote out of the sportswriters' hands, and Rose's
name was struck from the Hall of Fame ballot.*

Truth be told, Pete's managerial talents were marginal and the town had suffered through a series of mediocre seasons.

" IN THE EVENT OF SUDDEN DECOMPRESSION, OXYGEN MASKS WILL DROP DOWN.... CONTINUE TO BREATHE NORMALLY...."

New manager Lou Piniella threw temper tantrums and the occasional base as the team's superstars and superegos played themselves out. (The poster on the wall is an inside joke referring to a poster project I had just drawn identifying feelings.)

The Precinct used to be the place sports greats hung out. Now, it was the disabled list.

HIS TEAM DECIMATED BY INJURIES,
Lou Piniella MOTIONS FOR A PINCH HITTER

*Flame-throwing, hot-headed reliever Rob Dibble bruised a
first-grade teacher in the outfield red seats when he hurled a
ball into the stands in frustration after a game.*

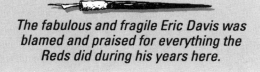

The fabulous and fragile Eric Davis was blamed and praised for everything the Reds did during his years here.

"NOW I'VE HEARD EVERYTHING.... OUR STAR OUTFIELDER RAN INTO AN OLD FRIEND YESTERDAY, AND WAS PLACED ON THE 21-DAY DISABLED LIST."

"...AND THAT BALL IS OUT OF HERE, FOLKS..., NO, WAIT A MINUTE....ERIC'S STILL GOING UP.....!"

A 15-year reunion of the Big Red Machine at the rebuilt Crosley Field in Blue Ash coincided with a powerful wire-to-wire 1990 season. Beating Pittsburgh in the playoffs, we suspected, would be our final highlight — we were to face the awesome A's.

GLORY DAYS

" ...(BOOP),...(BOOP),...(BOOP),... STEADY AS SHE GOES,...(BOOP),...(BOOP),...,"

"SEE YOU NEXT FALL."

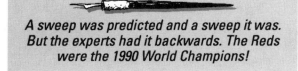

A sweep was predicted and a sweep it was. But the experts had it backwards. The Reds were the 1990 World Champions!

PUTTING US OUT OF OUR MISERY

Who Dey and Whyz Dat?

Six weeks into the Super Bowl season of '88, the Bengals were undefeated and rolling over anyone who got in their way. There was a feeling of invincibility in the air.

One day, as I was staring at a blank sheet of paper on my drawing board, I imagined a huge tiger sprawled across the football field, silent, menacing, absolutely impenetrable. I didn't bother getting out photos or researching anatomy as I usually do. The drawing was already complete in my mind and in an hour, it was complete on the paper. As an afterthought, I captioned it simply, "Next..."

When I came in the next morning, there were messages all over my desk. When would the sweat shirt come out? Where can we get the mug? Soon, banners of the drawing were appearing in the end zones and festooning the upper deck at Riverfront. By the time *The Enquirer* sent me to Miami to draw about the Super Bowl, it had become the unofficial symbol of the season and most of the players wore it emblazoned on their chests during press conferences.

I should have put that tiger out to stud but the next year, during an especially mediocre season, my cartoonist instincts took over. I aimed my pen at the emblem it had become and did everything I could to deflate it. It was peculiar to be popping my own balloon but, for once, I felt what it was like to be on the other end of my pen.

"NEED A LIFT?"

And you thought summer was hot in Cincinnati. In the fall, this place becomes a jungle.

"WELL, PHIL, I IMAGINE THIS SPELLS THE END OF THE ANNUAL FATHERS-SONS GAME....."

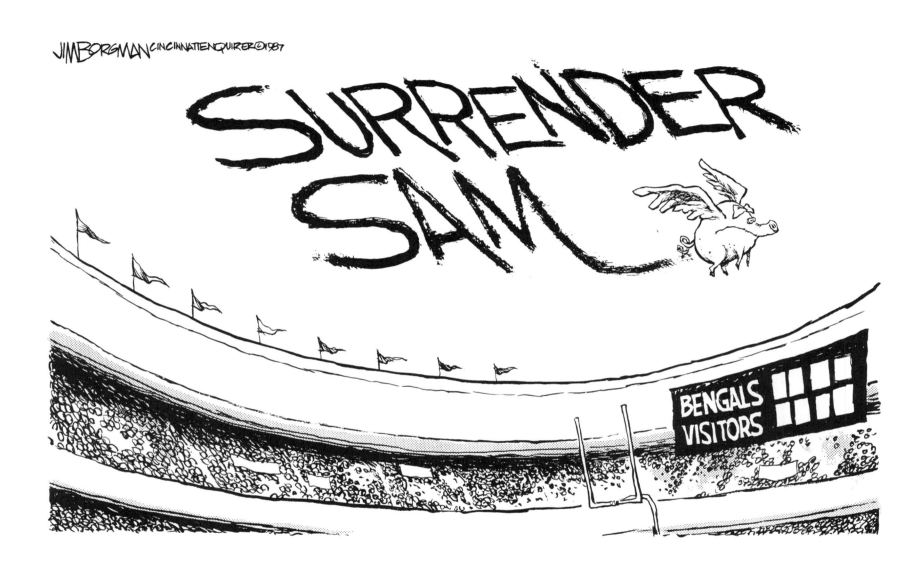

*By the end of 1987, Wyche's wicky-wacky style was
wearing thin with the fans, if not the management.*

"WARREN, YOU REALLY MUST STOP TAKING THE BENGALS' FORTUNES SO SERIOUSLY......"

"I HATE IT WHEN PHILBERT BREAKS INTO THE ICKEY SHUFFLE...."

NEXT....

Super Bowl-bound.

TOP
I found myself in Miami cartooning Super Bowl week the day George Bush was inaugurated.

BOTTOM
Running back Stanley Wilson had a drug relapse the night before the climactic game.

Stanley Wilson Tackled by Opponent

EYE OF THE TIGER

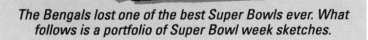

The Bengals lost one of the best Super Bowls ever. What follows is a portfolio of Super Bowl week sketches.

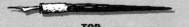

TOP
The last few years have been a roller coaster ride for the Bengals, with Wyche's mercurial personality grabbing most of the headlines.

BOTTOM
In one game, he took the microphone and reminded the unruly fans that they "didn't live in Cleveland." Shame on us.

"DON'T USE ALL THE HOT WATER...."

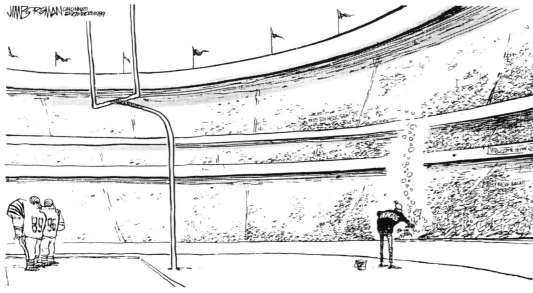

"....AND WE HAVE A BREAK IN THE ACTION WHILE SAM WYCHE WASHES A FAN'S MOUTH OUT WITH SOAP..."

134

"MARV, THE BENGALS ARE REALLY TAKING COACH WYCHE'S PEP TALK TO HEART HERE IN THE SECOND HALF...."

Off to a 3-13 season, Wyche told reporters that football is only a game. "Hey, there's golf to be played and tennis to be served up..."

TOP
No one made a T-shirt out of this one.

BOTTOM
*At one point, a WEBN DJ set up
housekeeping on a downtown
billboard, vowing not to come down
until the Bengals won a game. I forget.
Did he ever get down?*

NEXT...

ENTERTAINMENT DISTRICT

VOINOVICH VISIT

Your Tax Dollars at Work

We seem to split our time between feeling we're not getting anything for our tax dollars and complaining we're getting too much in the form of bureaucracy, waste, fraud and interference. We're told that three things are inevitable in this world: death, taxes and campaign commercials. Of the three, I'll take taxes.

I hesitate to draw cartoons about taxes for fear of spoiling your breakfast. The topic has an "Aw, what's the use" feel about it, and I can picture thousands of otherwise productive Cincinnatians crawling back to bed. For the sake of the Gross National Product, I lay off the subject when I can.

I drew a cartoon once in which a taxpayer was whittled away panel by panel ("...they took an arm and a leg in income taxes...Social Security took the shirt off my back...") until in the end his forlorn noggin was all that was left, laying on its side, saying, "Now I'm really worried. I hear they audit anyone who manages to come out ahead."

You know the feeling. Aw hell, let's go back to bed.

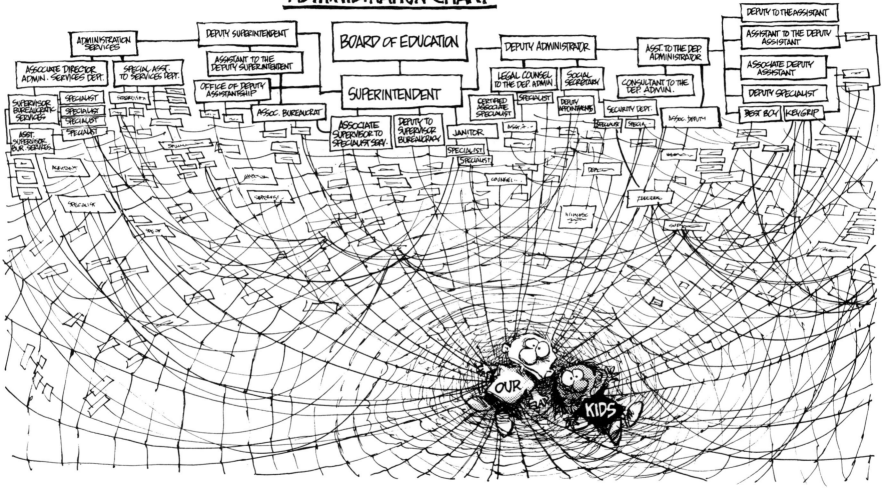

It's 9 a.m., where are your children? For most
Cincinnatians, the perception was building that the public
schools were a web of mismanagement.

"HANG IN THERE, KIDS.... WE'LL GET YOU THERE YET."

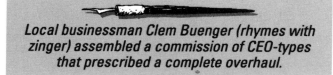

Local businessman Clem Buenger (rhymes with zinger) assembled a commission of CEO-types that prescribed a complete overhaul.

PARTY'S OVER!

Playing the role of martinet, Buenger and his commission provided the credibility taxpayers needed, and a levy was passed. The celebration was somewhat subdued.

TOP

Meanwhile, out at the Fernald Feed Plant they weren't making dog chow. With the Cold War over, the debate over cleaning up the incalculable leaks and storing the waste was heating up.

BOTTOM

A dramatic truck fire on I-71, just as the first shipment of thorium departed for a Nevada storage site, reminded us to hold our breath.

"ANOTHER LEAK OF RADIOACTIVE URANIUM WAS DISCOVERED AT FERNALD TODAY..."

Who says we're always behind the times? When Home State Savings and Loan locked its doors one day, it was a sign of things to come in the industry.

Head honcho Marvin Warner called himself the biggest victim of the collapse. Some might quibble with him.

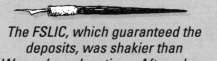

The FSLIC, which guaranteed the deposits, was shakier than Warner's explanations. After a long debate, the state concocted a bailout, but things just weren't the same.

"AS A MATTER OF FACT, I'D LIKE TO SEE SOME IDENTIFICATION FROM YOU, TOO."

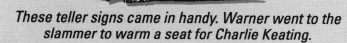
These teller signs came in handy. Warner went to the slammer to warm a seat for Charlie Keating.

149

"COWABUNGA! THIS SEWER'S NOT EVEN FIT FOR US MUTANTS!!"

Now what? The Enquirer *discovers the Hamilton County
sewer system is home to 17 times more toxic waste than
any other system in the state. Mondo notion.*

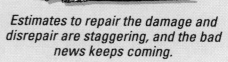

Estimates to repair the damage and disrepair are staggering, and the bad news keeps coming.

WAITING FOR IT TO HIT THE FAN

TESTS CONTINUE ON THE QUALITY OF OHIO RIVER WATER

152

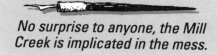

No surprise to anyone, the Mill Creek is implicated in the mess.

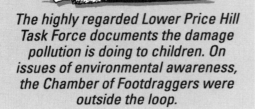

The highly regarded Lower Price Hill Task Force documents the damage pollution is doing to children. On issues of environmental awareness, the Chamber of Footdraggers were outside the loop.

GOVERNMENT RESPONSE TO POLLUTION POISONING

CANARY IN THE COALMINE

MELTDOWN!

Imagine the gall! Cincinnati Gas & Electric wanted us to pay for
their shoddy job on the never-licensed Zimmer nuclear time
bomb-turned-coal plant. Regulators upstate came to our defense.

"SPECIAL DELIVERY FROM CG&E..."

BARE BONES BUDGETING

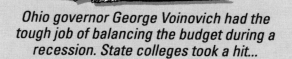

Ohio governor George Voinovich had the tough job of balancing the budget during a recession. State colleges took a hit...

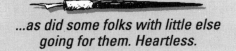

...as did some folks with little else going for them. Heartless.

159

"THE CAR TESTS FINE, BUT _HIS_ EXHAUST IS OFF THE SCALE!"

A series of bad air quality readings forced us to set up an auto emissions testing program. Fears of long lines and bureaucratic delays never materialized.

Our property tax bills are starting to look like the Manhattan phone book. Ever feel like you've been strung up by your thumbs?

The Mad Hatter's Tea Party

Not since Thomas Nast had Boss Tweed in Tammany Hall has a cartoonist had such ripe pickings as I have in the Hamilton County courthouse. I feel so blessed. I owe special thanks to the voters who inexplicably continue to throw the rascals back in.

Through disasters and tragedies at Drake Hospital and Allen House, jail fiascoes, cozy tax deals, nepotism and a drunk-driving commissioner, your loyal public servants schmoozed on the golf courses, double dipped and then complained about a 40-hour work week.

And Simon Leis thinks the crooks are in art museums.

Read on if you dare, but remember, we are through the looking glass here, people.

"HELLO, I'M A COUNTY TAXPAYER AND .... ER ...... YOU SEE, I'M LOOKING FOR ...... THAT IS, I'D LIKE TO TALK TO SOMEONE ABOUT....... I DEMAND AN EXPLANA— ...... OH, NEVER MIND. "

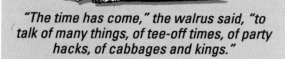

"The time has come," the walrus said, "to talk of many things, of tee-off times, of party hacks, of cabbages and kings."

"QUICK, GRAB THAT PHONE AND CALL AN EXORCIST!"

The Republicans have had control of the courthouse since before Joe DeCourcy made his first friend. The cracks in the foundation started showing on Party Boss Ralph Kohnen's watch.

The courts ruled the old workhouse suitable for only movie sets and *Shurf Lincoln* had to turn away any criminal without a reservation at the new Justice Center.

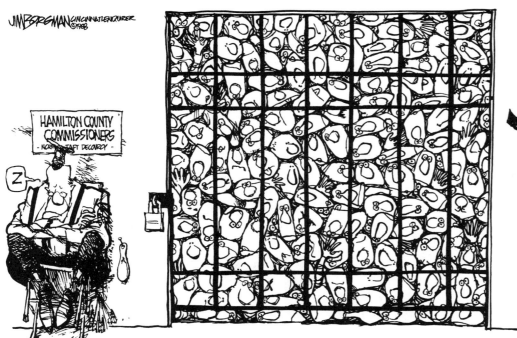

JIM BORGMAN CINCINNATI ENQUIRER ©1988

HAMILTON COUNTY COMMISSIONERS
- NORM TAFT DECONCY -

JAIL ←

167

Turns out if you were an F.O.J. (friend of county auditor Joe DeCourcy), you might just have one of the lower tax bills in town.

"JEEMINY! THEY'RE STILL HERE! MAYBE WE WEREN'T WISHING HARD ENOUGH!"

Commissioners Murdock, Taft and young Joe DeCourcy. Tweedledee, Tweedledum and Tweedledumber. Bad stuff was happening at the county home for kids who had enough trouble already.

Sentence first, verdict afterwards. Off with their heads! News crews caught your public servants inspecting the fairways...on your tab.

JUST WEEDING OUT THE BAD ONES

When Democratic DJ Dusty Rhodes was elected
county auditor, courthouse cronies found a
whole lotta shakin' going on.

A mysterious odor in the county office building was
sending workers home sick. Curiouser and curiouser.

SALT and PEPPER HAIR

BOBBIE STERNE

SCOTT JOHNSON

ARN PORSH

Who's Who and Who's Not

Cincinnati loves to list its luminaries, homegrown celebrities who have made their mark like Roy Rogers, Rosemary Clooney, Doris Day and, um, Charles Manson. Steven Spielberg passed though town once on a Cub Scout field trip so we figure we can claim him, too. Also Annie Oakley and any number of obese and ineffective presidents.

Someday, you should visit our Has-Been Hall of Fame near Kings Island. Follow the arrows or follow the cars.

A great doughy face is a cartoonist's dream and this town produces them by the truckload. Give me John Mirlisena, Marge Schott or Dave Mann over any three heartthrobs you can name. But it's a good heart and a Midwestern sense of humor that make our local heroes special to us. Most of the characters we hold dear wouldn't be recognized on the streets of any other town, and that's just fine with us.

Besides, Hollywood's beating down our door to get in.

For all Sam Wyche's whining, it was a joy to have a coach
who thought about more than football. In off-hours, he
worked for the homeless. God bless you, Sam.

DESIGN FOR A MONUMENT

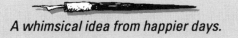
A whimsical idea from happier days.

" ....AND I SUPPOSE YOU'RE NORMA RASHID!"

Channel 5 stuck a phony beard on Jerry Springer to
disguise him for an undercover look at life on the streets.

... AND THOSE YOU DON'T SEE.

Nick Clooney left town as one of Cincinnati's best-loved news voices. As happens when we're lucky, he found his way back home.

CINCINNATI MONUMENT

L.D. WARREN

CINCINNATI ENQUIRER '92
THANKS L.D.

L.D. Warren, The Cincinnati Enquirer's editorial cartoonist for 33 years, owned the hearts of many Cincinnatians and certainly mine. L.D. recommended me for this job when I felt I wasn't even worthy to carry his ink bottle. An era ended when he passed away.

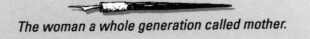

The woman a whole generation called mother.

"I STILL DON'T SEE WHAT'S SO OFFENSIVE ABOUT THESE CHARACTERS, DO YOU, BOOGERFLICKER?"

Whose bright idea was this nauseating toy line from Kenner? As a dad with two impressionable kids under 10, I was really annoyed.

After years of trying to quash devil-worship rumors surrounding its logo, Procter & Gamble broke down and redesigned it.

JIM BORGMAN CINCINNATI ENQUIRER©1988

BIG KLU
1924-1988

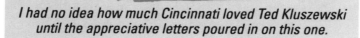

I had no idea how much Cincinnati loved Ted Kluszewski
until the appreciative letters poured in on this one.

" .... NEXT UP, A LOOK AT THE WEATHER WITH GUY GUCKENBERGER. "

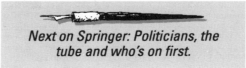

*Next on Springer: Politicians, the
tube and who's on first.*

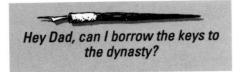

Hey Dad, can I borrow the keys to the dynasty?

The TORCH IS PASSED

"LOOKS TO ME LIKE EITHER ONE WOULD FIT INTO CONGRESS JUST FINE...."

"ORDER IN THE COURT! ORDER IN THE COURT! ......OOOPS, SORRY, BUT SOMEBODY HAD TO SAY IT...!.."

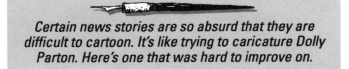

Certain news stories are so absurd that they are difficult to cartoon. It's like trying to caricature Dolly Parton. Here's one that was hard to improve on.

DEATH'S FACE

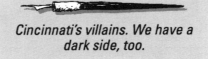

Cincinnati's villains. We have a dark side, too.

189

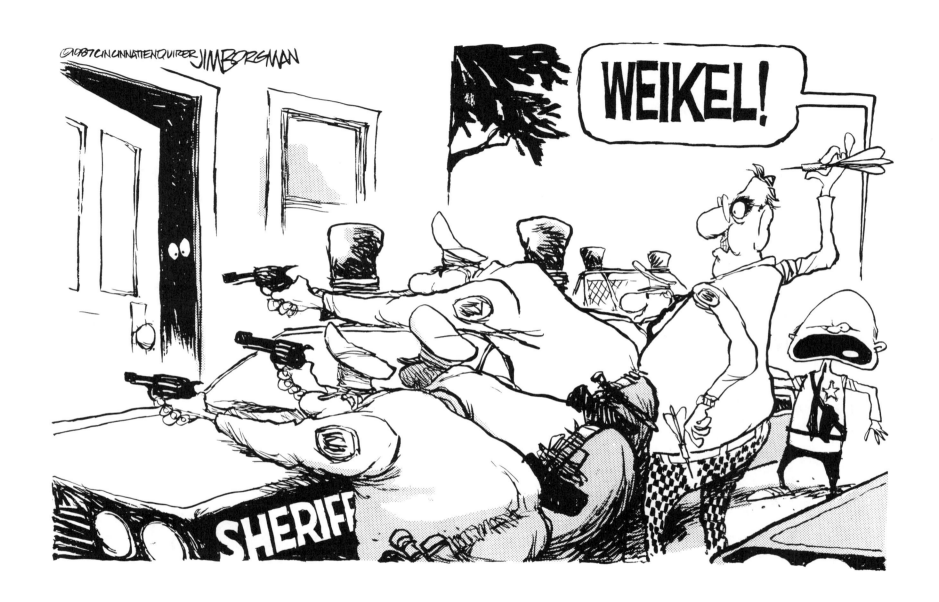

As an Enquirer *columnist, Frank Weikel bestowed "darts and flowers" on the city's two-bit newsmakers before being hired by Sheriff Simon Leis' department.*

GONNA ROUND THIRD JUST A LITTLE MORE GINGERLY FOR AWHILE...

When veteran Reds announcer Joe Nuxhall
went on the D.L. before the '92 season, he
learned just how much the town loved him.

The Dave Shula era began under the worst of circumstances:
an opening game in Seattle, site of a looming court fight over
rape allegations against 20 Bengals.

PAUL BROWN 1908·1991

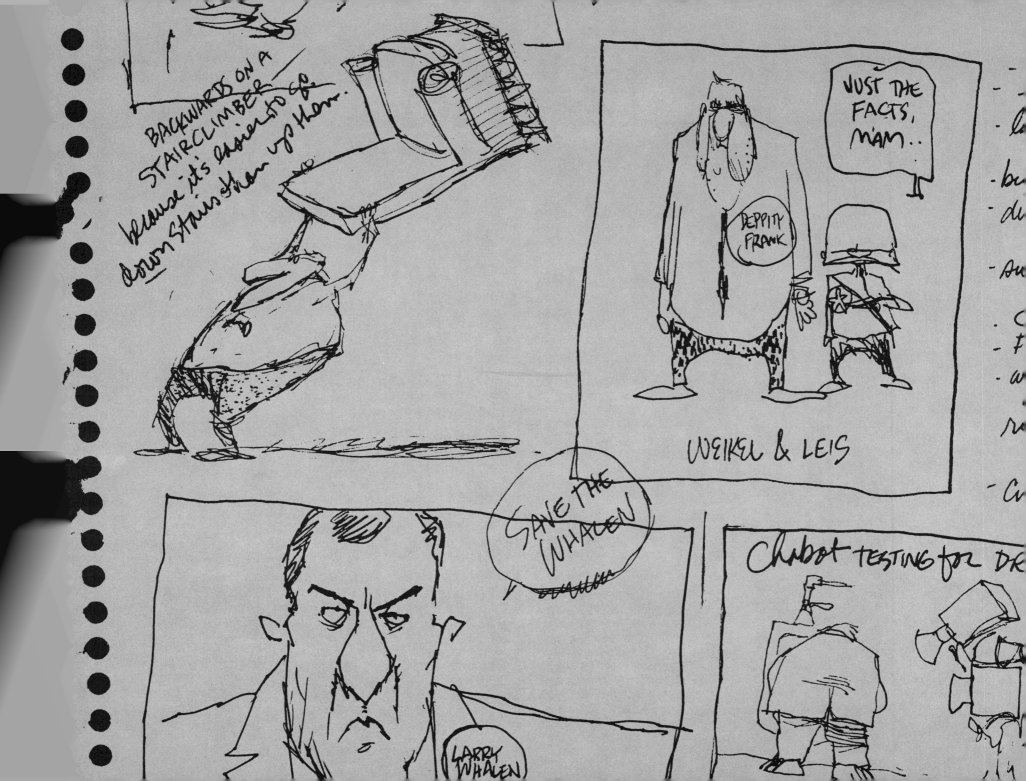

You Can't Do That in Cincinnati

Cincinnati has had a long and well, let's face it, disastrous relationship with the arts which started long before Bobby Mapplethorpe was a strange little boy. We have produced dozens of great, cutting-edge artists like Jim Dine, for example, who have run off screaming to New York and who wouldn't come back to Cincinnati if you commissioned them.

When Cincinnati does foray into the creative unknown, the results can be embarrassing. Witness our expensive Fountain Square sculpture and late-night urinal, "Law and Society," recently relocated and now proudly displayed under the Brent Spence Bridge, visible whenever the river is low.

Our dubious affair with the muses may trace back to the fact that, as a city, we tend to cinch up our pants a bit tight. Our Germanic heritage must have something to do with it. A sense of order can be comforting, but if you find yourself waiting for the 'Don't Walk' sign to turn at 3 a.m., you might want to have that looked at.

"**THERE'S** THE OLD CINCINNATI 'CAN'T DO' SPIRIT!"

In my almost two decades at The Enquirer *as a cartoonist, I have seen the legality and morality of everything from yard sales to pooper scoopers debated. City Council goes on these regulation jags. This one had to do with tailgate-party cuisine.*

"SMOKING IN A PUBLIC CUBICLE, CARRYING A CONCEALED TIPARILLO, AND UNLAWFULLY ATTEMPTING TO FLICK A BIC ....BOOK HIM."

When the hazards of passive smoke became known, whole buildings became smoke-free zones in Cincinnati, including our new *Enquirer* building. That's big news in our business.

"... AND AS A FINAL EMERGENCY PRECAUTION, WE HAVE ARRANGED TO HAVE A PSYCHIATRIST STANDING BY AT ALL TIMES."

" ME? I WAS CAUGHT BUYING A 'HUSTLER' AT A YARD SALE WHILE SMOKING A CIGARETTE AND WALKING MY PIT BULL WITHOUT A POOPER SCOOPER."

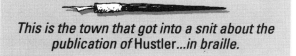

This is the town that got into a snit about the publication of Hustler...in braille.

"...SO I SEZ TO DAT PUNK, SEZ I, 'YOU JUST WAIT, MISTER HIGH-AND-MIGHTY COUNCILMAN... SOMEDAY I'M GONNA GET SPRUNG FROM DAT COOLER, AND YOU'LL REGRET DE DAY YOU EVER TANGLED WID OLD BOWZER, YOU WILL....'"

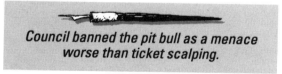

Council banned the pit bull as a menace
worse than ticket scalping.

" IT'S THE NEW SHERIFF, BOYS! HIDE THE GIRLIE MAGAZINES!"

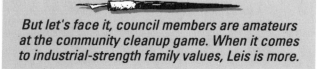

But let's face it, council members are amateurs at the community cleanup game. When it comes to industrial-strength family values, Leis is more.

Great Moments in AMERICAN Thought...

The debate turns serious for me when the forces of constriction suffocate my right to make reasonable choices. The Mapplethorpe exhibit was certainly a look at the dark side of humanity, but that is an aspect of life some of us choose to grapple with.

"I TOLD YOU THAT EXHIBIT WOULD UNDERMINE OUR COMMUNITY VALUES, EDNA!"

The would-be censors ensured throngs of visitors for the controversial exhibit. By the end of their protest, Cincinnatians knew the work of Robert Mapplethorpe in intimate detail.

"FRANKLY, THERE'S SO MUCH OBSCENITY AROUND HERE TO CONSIDER, I DON'T HAVE TIME FOR A SILLY LITTLE ART SHOW."

Meanwhile, the real pornography thrives.

The Mapplethorpe controversy caught the national spotlight and galvanized Cincinnati's puritanical image. You want Renaissance men? Go to Italy. The only Florence these guys know is Florence Mall.

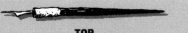

TOP
Dennis Barrie, Contemporary Arts Center director, was toasted as a hero in the art world but the CAC's membership surge lasted only for a year...

BOTTOM
...and some wondered about the dampening effect the whole affair would have on getting other cutting-edge shows to town.

"I MISS MAPPLETHORPE."

"IT'S A CHALLENGING SHOW — I DON'T KNOW HOW THEY SNUCK IT PAST THE CENSORS..."

ANOTHER WILD GOOSE CHASE COMES TO NOUGHT

The jury threw the case out on its ear in a matter of minutes and Shurf Leis was sent home sputtering.

"YOU ARE ALL UNDER ARREST.."

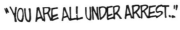

"SHERIFF LEIS, IF YOU DON'T MIND,....."